CPS-Morrill E.S.

3488000002535 8

Royston, Angela   613.7 ROY
Get some rest!

 W9-BCI-652

DATE DUE

613.7   BC#34880000025358 $25.36
ROY   Royston, Angela
               Get some rest!

                    Morrill E.S.
                Chicago Public Schools
            1431 North Leamington Avenue
                  Chicago, IL 60651

Look After Yourself

Get Some Rest!

Angela Royston

Heinemann Library
Chicago, Illinois

© 2003 Heinemann Library
a division of Reed Elsevier Inc.
Chicago, Illinois

All rights reserved. No part of this publication may be reproduced or transmitted in any form or by any means, electronic or mechanical, including photocopying, recording, taping, or any information storage and retrieval system, without permission in writing from the publisher.

Designed by Dave Oakley
Photo research by Helen Reilly
Originated by Dot Gradations Ltd
Printed and bound in China by South China Printing Company

07 06 05 04 03
10 9 8 7 6 5 4 3 2 1

Library of Congress Cataloging-in-Publication Data
Royston, Angela.
  Get some rest! / Angela Royston.
    v. cm. -- (Look after yourself)
Includes bibliographical references and index.
Contents: Your body -- Rest and recover -- Relaxing after exercise
 -- Give your brain a break! -- Sleep -- Getting enough sleep --
Relaxing before bed -- Early to bed, early to rise -- Getting overtired
 -- Broken sleep -- Bad dreams -- Extra rest -- It's a fact.
  ISBN 1-4034-4442-0 (libr. bdg.) -- ISBN 1-4034-4451-X (pbk.)
1. Rest--Juvenile literature. [1. Rest. 2. Sleep.] I. Title.
  RA785.R69 2003
  613.7'9--dc21
                              2003000992
Acknowledgments
The author and publisher are grateful to the following for permission to reproduce copyright material:
Cover photograph by Kwame Zikomo/SuperStock.
pp. 4, 8 Powerstock; p. 5 Lucy Tizard/Bubbles; pp. 6, 7, 15, 18, 19, 22, 23, 27 Trevor Clifford; p. 9 Frans Rombout/Bubbles; pp. 10, 21, 26 Photodisc; p. 11 Peter Hince/Getty Images; pp. 12, 17 S. Grant/Trip; p. 13 David Roth/Getty Images; p. 14 Gaillard, Jerrican/Science Photo Library; p. 16 White Packert/Getty Images; p. 20 Mark Clarke/Science Photo Library; p. 24 Jo Makin/Last Resort; p. 25 Ian West/Bubbles.

Special thanks to David Wright for his help in the preparation of this book.

Every effort has been made to contact copyright holders of any material reproduced in this book. Any omissions will be rectified in subsequent printings if notice is given to the publisher.

Some words are shown in bold, **like this.** You can find out what they mean by looking in the glossary.

Contents

Your Body

Your body is made up of many different parts that work together. The **muscles** in your arms and legs work together to make a swing go higher and faster.

4

It takes lots of **energy** for your body and your brain to work. Resting your mind and your body will help you stay healthy.

5

Exercise is good for your body, but you also need to rest. After you have been running fast, you may feel tired and **out of breath.**

6

Your **muscles** have been working hard, and so have your **heart** and **lungs.** If you sit down for a few minutes, these parts of your body can **recover.**

Relaxing after Exercise

It takes lots of **energy** to climb and walk. It can make your body very tired. It can also make the **muscles** in your legs ache.

After **exercising** hard, you may just want to rest. Playing a quiet game is one good way to rest your body.

Give Your Brain a Break!

When you work hard at school, you have to **concentrate.** You use your **brain** to think, and thinking makes you tired. Sometimes your brain needs to **relax,** too!

At recess, you can go outside to play. Playing is a good way to rest your brain.

Sleep

When you go to sleep at night, you rest your body and your **brain.** Your **muscles** rest. Your brain and your body **recover** from the day.

12

Other parts of your body slow down when you sleep. Your **heart** beats more slowly. You breathe more deeply. When you wake up, your whole body feels rested and full of **energy.**

13

Getting Enough Sleep

If you do not get enough sleep, you might wake up feeling tired. You might also become tired during the day. It is hard to **concentrate** when you are tired.

If you are very tired, you may feel grouchy. You may not enjoy playing with your friends. You need about ten hours of sleep every night.

Relaxing Before Bed

Many people take a bath each night before bed. The hot water helps them **relax.** Doing the same thing every night can be a **routine** that helps you get to sleep.

You are more likely to fall asleep if you are relaxed. Reading a story before you go to sleep is a good way to relax. Listening to music is relaxing, too.

Early to Bed, Early to Rise

Your body gets used to going to sleep at a certain time every night. Having a **routine** bedtime can help you sleep better.

18

Most people also wake up at about the same time every morning. If you have had enough sleep, you will find it easy to wake up.

19

Getting Overtired

On special days, you may stay up late. But staying up late too often may break your **routine.** You may become **overtired** and upset.

When you stay up late, your **brain** is awake for too long. Even though you may be tired, your brain has a hard time slowing down.

Broken Sleep

You may wake up in the middle of the night. You may wake up because you are sick. Or you may need to go to the bathroom.

You may wake up because you are thirsty. Keep a glass of water beside your bed. A drink of water may help you get back to sleep.

Bad Dreams

Most people sleep better in a dark room. But sometimes ordinary things look scary in the dark. So, some people like to sleep with a night-light on.

24

Everyone has bad dreams from time to time. Bad dreams can make you feel scared. Sometimes you need an adult to tell you that your dreams are not real.

Extra Rest

When you are sick, you usually sleep more. Sometimes you may stay asleep all day. Your body is using lots of **energy** to fight **germs.** This may make you feel tired.

When you get better, you may want to sit up. Even then, you should get lots of rest. Resting helps your body get well more quickly.

It's a Fact!

Your body cannot **digest** food very well when you are asleep. You may get **indigestion** and this can give you bad dreams. Avoid eating a large meal just before you go to bed.

Feeling hungry can keep you awake at night. It is best to eat the last meal of the day three or four hours before you go to bed. A small snack just before bedtime can help you sleep.

A warm drink can also help you get to sleep. A drink of warm milk, hot chocolate, or **herb** tea can make you feel **relaxed** and help you fall asleep.

Avoid drinks that may keep you awake. Some cola, tea, and coffee contain a drug called **caffeine.** Caffeine wakes up your **brain** and may keep you from sleeping.

The first few hours of sleep are the deepest. Most people have three, four, or five dreams each night. You may only remember a dream if you wake up in the middle of it.

Sleep is important for giving you a healthy mind as well as a healthy body. People who have not slept for more than three days cannot think clearly. They begin to see and hear things that are not there.

Glossary

brain   part of the body that controls the whole body and allows you to be aware of things

caffeine   drug that wakes up the brain and makes you feel more alert. Some tea, coffee, and cola contain caffeine.

concentrate   to think hard about one thing

digest   when your stomach breaks down food after eating

energy   power to do work or move about

exercise   activity that makes your muscles work hard

germ   tiny living thing that attacks different parts of your body; a germ can cause sickness

heart   part of the body that pumps blood around the rest of the body

herb   plant that can be used to flavor food, make medicine, or make tea

indigestion   when your stomach or intestines feel swollen or painful after eating

lung   part of the body that takes in oxygen from the air you breathe in

muscle   part of the body that tightens, or contracts, to move a bone or other part of the body

out of breath   panting or gasping for air

overtired   too tired

recover   to get back to normal

relax   to rest your body and mind

routine   doing something the same way all the time or at the same time every day

More Books to Read

Feeney, Kathy. *Sleep Well: You Need to Rest.* Mankato, Minn.: Capstone Press, 2001.

Gordon, Sharon. *A Good Night's Sleep.* Danbury, Conn.: Children's Press, 2002.

Royston, Angela. *A Healthy Body.* Chicago: Heinemann Library, 1999.

Index